For those interested in  nan
flourishing, Dwight Vogt' ... ? to
begin. It is written in a cle... ..., ... personal manner. Dwight has
over 30 years of working as a project manager, country director, and
executive leader for an international development organization. One of
the strengths of this book is that Dwight is telling his personal story of
what he has learned from experience and reflection. Come join him on
this journey. I highly recommend *Made to Flourish*.

— **Darrow Miller**, Author, Co-founder,
Disciple Nations Alliance

Made to Flourish is a fresh, clean look at God's good intentions for his
creation, and the role he invites us to enter into with him on behalf of all
individuals, communities, and nations. I've known and worked with
Dwight Vogt for more than 35 years and would expect nothing less than
what he's delivered in this short gem of a biblical and personal reflection.
It's "biblical worldview" made practical – thanks, Dwight!

— **Dave Conner**, Ed.D., SPHR, ACC,
Director of Talent Development, Duke University Development

My good friend and former colleague has written a much needed and
very poignant book on God's whole intent for all humans to fully
flourish. In the United States, reference is often made to certain
evangelical churches as being "full gospel" due to their emphasis on
spiritual gifts. But Dwight Vogt rightly shows what it means to be full
gospel in this great treatise. I highly recommend it.

— **David Evans**, Senior Director for Innovation,
World Vision International

Dwight gently provides the wisdom revealing God's intention for our lives and how this spreads into our community, our country, and the world that He has created. His words challenge us to live as our God created us to live, flourishing as we reflect the One whose image we bear.

— **Gene Mildren**, President, Mildren Design Group, P.C.

Dwight Vogt gives voice to our longing for wholeness, and the tension we feel between what is and what could be in society. Going back to God's original plan for mankind, he calls us to represent the kingdom of God in every facet of modern culture.

— **Peggy Arendt**, Member, ReachGlobal,
Evangelical Free Church of America (EFCA)

The beauty of *Made to Flourish* is that it focuses on what we, as God's people, have been *saved to*. While Dwight is straightforward in presenting what we have been *saved from* he also lays out what we have been *saved to* in a clear and compelling manner. Dwight allows us to see the key truths we need to embrace and live out in all arenas of our lives. So as citizens, workers, family members, neighbors, whatever the collection of hats one wears, *Made to Flourish* is a simple yet powerful call to redeem the opportunities God is giving us.

— **Steve Corbett**, Coauthor of *When Helping Hurts*,
Associate Professor of Community Development at Covenant College

In *Made to Flourish*, Dwight Vogt draws our attention back to God's original intention for the human race. God's heart is for all to flourish—to have wholeness and deep satisfaction. In spite of how far we have fallen, there is hope. Dwight leads us through the steps to return to God's loving plan.

— **Faith Cummings**, M.Div.,
Pastor of Women's Ministry, Living Streams Christian Church

MADE TO FLOURISH

GOD'S DESIGN FOR ALL INDIVIDUALS, COMMUNITIES, AND NATIONS

DWIGHT VOGT

Made to Flourish: God's Design for All Individuals, Communities, and Nations
Copyright ©2017 by Dwight Vogt

All rights reserved. No part of this book may be reproduced in any form without permission in writing from the publisher, except in the case of brief quotations in critical articles or reviews.

Published by the Disciple Nations Alliance
1110 E. Missouri Avenue, Suite 393
Phoenix, Arizona, 85014
www.disciplenations.org

Cover design: Lisa Lewis
Layout: Penoaks Publishing

ISBN: 0692930663
ISBN 13: 9780692930663

Unless shown otherwise all scripture quotations are from the ESV® Bible (The Holy Bible, English Standard Version®), copyright © 2001 by Crossway, a publishing ministry of Good News Publishers. Used by permission. All rights reserved.

Acknowledgments

Several years ago my wife Deborah and I were hiking around a lake in northern Arizona, and she asked me to share my "work" thoughts. After my lengthy response, Deborah said, "You should write this down," and those thoughts became the outline for this book. She has been encouraging me in the process ever since by listening, reading drafts, and giving input. I am immensely grateful to her. Thank you, dear.

I appreciate the support and encouragement of my colleague Scott Allen, who has given me time and resources. I am grateful to Darrow Miller for helping me to start thinking about this topic years ago with his teachings in *The Development Ethic*.[1]

I also wish to acknowledge Stan Guthrie for his extensive help in organizing my first draft and Gary Brumbelow for his editing support.

---

1   Darrow L. Miller, *The Development Ethic* (Food for the Hungry International, 1988), http://www.disciplenations.org/media/Development-Ethic-Hope-for-a-Culture-of-Poverty_Miller.pdf

Contents

"...but the righteous will flourish like a green leaf."

— *Proverbs 11:28*

PART 1
The Disconnect between the Gospel and Development

We all want to progress and see life get better. Parents all over the world want their children to lead a better life than they have led. We wake up in the morning and hope today is better than yesterday.

This desire to develop—to grow and make things better—is innate. It is wired into us. A healthy newborn instinctively begins growing and progressing. She quickly starts looking, listening, learning, and exercising. Soon she is swirling her cereal around in her bowl to make a design. Next she is placing one toy block on top of another to build something. We are wired to develop by our great Creator, who does nothing in vain.

Whether we're talking about individuals or communities or nations, people want to grow and progress. They want to develop. At its essence, development is about making life better. It is about people overcoming life's challenges and improving their lives in sustainable ways.

For some this looks like getting a clean water supply near or even inside their home. For others it means gaining a new skill to improve their work. For someone else it's overcoming an addiction. For another it might be going to graduate school to increase one's knowledge and ability. For a business owner, it may involve growing sales. For a community it might be lowering the crime rate or increasing business activity.

A good synonym for *develop* is *flourish*. To *flourish* means to grow and develop in a particularly healthy and vigorous way. It's the tree covered with green leaves and loaded with good fruit. It's the child learning and excelling at school. It's the craftsman using his skills to build a quality product. It's the amazing picture of creation we see in Genesis 1 and 2.

The summer after my senior year of college, I traveled with a large team of students and several faculty members to Thailand to work with refugees from Laos, Cambodia, Vietnam, and Myanmar. In August the team returned to the United States, but I stayed. One opportunity led to another, and international development work eventually became my vocational focus and has remained such for more than thirty years.

My vocation has given me reason to think long and hard about this topic, to ask, "What does it mean to truly flourish, and how can we best help individuals and communities to develop and progress?"

As a Christian I have often asked myself how the Bible and its comprehensive worldview speak to development. We are told "Do not love the world or the things in the world" (1 John 2:15). How does this fit? More specifically, how does development fit into the gospel?

I don't think I am alone in asking these questions. How does this seemingly innate desire to make life better—to develop and flourish—fit into God's plan...or does it?

We often sense that the Christian faith actually calls for the opposite. We assume that the ideal Christian is a type of Mother

Teresa, who forsakes material goods and health and serves the poor full-time. Or we sense the ideal is someone like the Apostle Paul, who earns only enough to feed himself and gives his life to traveling the world preaching and teaching. We hear sayings from Jesus that seem to point in the opposite direction of flourishing.

- "Blessed are you who are poor, for yours is the kingdom of God" (Luke 6:20).
- "But woe to you who are rich for you have received your consolation" (Luke 6:24).
- "Foxes have holes, and birds of the air have nests, but the Son of Man has nowhere to lay his head" (Matt. 8:20).
- "If anyone would come after me, let him deny himself and take up his cross daily and follow me" (Luke 9:23).

The truth is, Jesus *does* call us to follow him and in so doing calls us to embrace hardship and struggle as it comes. The experience of suffering and evil in this broken world is real. Good people suffer pain and loss. Saints are martyred. Life is difficult. Jesus gave no illusions that life would be all rosy for the God-fearing. There are times when the best we can do is to endure well and not run.

But are suffering and hardship in opposition to flourishing? When I was young we planted a new tree in our yard and securely staked it to protect it from the wind. Several years later we removed the stake and the tree bent completely over at the first breeze. A tree's trunk goes stronger because of the wind. Its roots go deeper because of drought. Its branches produce more fruit when pruned.

James 1 and John 15 speak of how hardship works in our lives to produce flourishing. Jesus suffered above all others, but he also flourished in life beyond all others. Stephen the first martyr suffered in death, but he lived an amazingly fruitful life marked by great wisdom, courage, and power.[1] Our family suffered the loss of our second daughter, which was confusing at the time, yet we have experienced a level of flourishing in our lives that would not have been possible apart from that journey.

Some see the connection between development and the gospel in the social gospel, which asserts that the transformation of society and the coming of the kingdom of God are accomplished through education and law, public policy, and economic policy. Supporters of the social gospel regard material salvation as superior to spiritual salvation. This is a fundamental denial of the gospel.

Others see the connection between flourishing and the gospel in the prosperity gospel, which asserts that health and material wealth are always the will of God. These blessings are guaranteed to those who exercise faith, positive confessions, and financial giving to the church (or a Christian leader). This approach essentially views the Bible as a contract between God and humans; if humans have faith in God and obey him in certain ways, God will deliver security, health, and prosperity.

Both the social gospel and the prosperity gospel, with their particular emphases on the implications of the good news and the attitudes required to obtain them, fail to see the legitimate connection between development and the gospel.

To understand how development fits into the gospel, we need to start in Genesis. This is where the gospel story begins.

Every philosophy and religion in the world aims to provide an understanding of life and the world, a way to make sense of the primary relationships of life, shown as follows:

---

1   Acts 6–7.

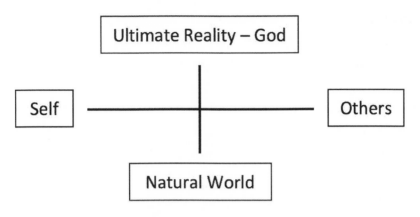

The primary relationships of life

Religion and philosophy seek to address the basic questions about life.

- Is there a spiritual reality? If so, what is it?
- What does it mean to be human?
- What is our relationship to the natural world?
- What is our purpose? Why are we here?
- What are the rules to live by? Who sets them?
- Why is there suffering and evil? How should we respond to them?

We consciously or unconsciously assign answers to these questions, and those answers become the basic assumptions by which we live our lives. We may even take answers from multiple religions, philosophies, and ideas. We call this set of answers a worldview. It is how we understand the world and our life. Everyone has a worldview. Our worldview is like a pair of eyeglasses we wear on the mind through which we interpret life and decide what is true and real. Literal eyeglasses help us see the world accurately or, if the prescription is wrong, they distort our view. Likewise a worldview can bring clarity or it can distort and prevent us from seeing the world as it truly is. It may be right or wrong.

The Bible gives us a comprehensive worldview and a clear window into reality. As my colleague Darrow Miller says, the biblical worldview alone fully comports with reality—"reality as it really is." It reveals God's design for the world and everything in it. It reveals who we are and why we are here on this planet. It addresses every aspect of our lives.

The Bible answers the basic worldview questions—the basic questions about life—in the first three chapters.

Genesis 1 and 2 give us God's design at creation for how the world was to be and function. It spells out our vocation. Chapter 3 tells us what went wrong and explains our current experience of life. It shows how our vocation was corrupted.

Genesis 1 & 2	Genesis 3
God's design at creation	What went wrong
God's original intentions	Our current reality
Our vocation	Our vocation corrupted

The question is, do we build our worldview understanding on chapters 1 and 2—how God designed the world and mankind to be? Or do we build it on chapter 3—how the world is today?

The right answer is "both," but here is where I unknowingly missed something critical. My Christian worldview was framed primarily by what went wrong in Genesis 3 and not by God's original design for our lives and vocation in chapters 1 and 2.

I was raised in an evangelical church environment, attending worship services, Sunday school, Vacation Bible School, Bible clubs, and summer camps. The theological instruction I received from these emphasized chapter 3 without fully considering chapters 1 and 2. As a result my understanding of God's purposes was incomplete, and early on in my work I struggled to see the connection between development—God's purposes for human flourishing—and the gospel.

I grew up with the *Roman Road to Salvation*, the *Wordless Book*, and the *Four Spiritual Laws*. The *Roman Road* summarizes the gospel in five verses from the book of Romans. The first verse is Romans 3:23, which says, "For all have sinned and fall short of the glory of God." The *Wordless Book* represents the key points of the gospel in five colored pages. The first page is gold, which is to remind us of heaven—God wants everyone to be with him in heaven. The second page is dark, which reminds us of the darkness of sin—for all have sinned. The *Four Spiritual Laws* begins with the statement "God loves you and has a wonderful plan for your life" and then points to our separation from God as a result of our sin.

These well-known evangelism tools give a simple and compelling summary of the gospel. All of them rightly emphasize the reality of our sin, how it separates us from God, and how, apart from Christ, we are all under judgment. But none of them point back to God's original intentions for our lives and for creation in Genesis 1 and 2.

These tools make clear how Jesus Christ atoned for our sin on the cross so that we can be forgiven, be set free from sin and shame, have a personal relationship with God, and go to be with him in heaven when we die. They make clear that we are saved by grace alone—not by works—and that we must individually believe and receive this gift of salvation. God gives us the Holy Spirit to help us and as a seal of his salvation. I understood that in response we are to live lives that glorify God, and we are to share this gospel with others so that they can have eternal life and a relationship with God as well.

It was also clear to me from Scripture that God cared about the physical, economic, and social needs of people, and that Christ's death on the cross was for the reconciliation of *all* things (Col. 1:20).

This was my understanding of the gospel. My understanding of how this applied to development or working to improve the conditions of life was as follows:

- People needed to know that God loves them. They needed to hear this message of salvation so they could have forgiveness of sin, a relationship with God, and the assurance of eternal life with God in heaven. Doing development work or helping them improve their lives was a way to show them God's love so that they could respond to his message.
- When we served others by helping them improve their lives, we glorified and pleased God.
- Finally, I understood that when people believed in God and obeyed him they could expect his blessing. This blessing would lead to the development of their lives physically, socially, and economically.

All of this is true, and for about twenty years this was my understanding of how development connected to the gospel.

So what was I missing? *Because my understanding of God's purposes and gospel began in Genesis 3, I did not see God's original intentions and vocation for mankind in Genesis 1 and 2 and how the gospel connected to this.*

For example, one of the worldview questions is about humanity. What is my identity? Who am I? What is my relationship to God? The gospel understanding I grew up with answered this question from Genesis 3. Man is a fallen sinner—"For all have sinned"[2] and "There is none righteous, no not one."[3] This is true, and it is definitely our present experience. But when we answer this question from Genesis 1, we see that we are created in the likeness of God—male and female (Gen. 1:27). God established our human identity as his image-bearers. As an image-bearer every person is to reflect God's character and nature to one another and to all creation. We know this identity was broken and devastated by sin (Gen. 3), but God does not change his mind. This is still his design for every person. The saving work of Jesus Christ is about restoring this identity to people (1 Cor. 15:49; Heb. 2:9–18). Theologian N. T. Wright refers to this as being made "fully human."[4]

Development is about helping people live fully as God's image-bearers. This "development" is only possible through Christ. This is why if we are to engage in helping people improve their lives and truly flourish they need Christ.

A second example of what is missed when we begin the gospel in Genesis 3 concerns the worldview question about our relationship to the natural world. What is our relationship to nature or to the world in general? When this is answered in Genesis 3, the relationship between humans and the natural world is marked by conflict and struggle. Women endure pain in childbirth. The ground produces thorns and thistles; we grow food only by hard, sweat-producing labor. We do well to survive and persevere until we die.

---

2 Romans 3:23.

3 Romans 3:10 (KJV).

4 N. T. Wright, "How Can the Bible Be Authoritative?" (Vox Evangelica, 1991), 7–32, http://ntwrightpage.com/2016/07/12/how-can-the-bible-be-authoritative/.

This is true, but when we begin the gospel from Genesis 1, we see God created mankind to rule over creation and to be fruitful and fill the earth. God's purpose for all people is not just to survive and endure until death. It is to rule over all creation and all that this implies. Because of sin everyone falls far short of this vocation, but this is still God's purpose for our lives. The saving work of Jesus Christ includes restoring this divine vocation to every person.

How this fits with development is clear. God's plan is that people rule over creation to fill the earth and make it flourish. Performing this vocation fully as God intended is only possible through Christ.

A third example of what is missed when we begin the gospel in Genesis 3 concerns the question of God's relationship to this world. In Genesis 3 we see a world that is under the curse, broken by sin, and separated from God. This is true. But when we begin the gospel in Genesis 1, we see that God created a world that was perfect, "very good," and he was present in it. In other words, heaven and earth were united. *Then* sin entered and with it separation and death. The story of the Bible—the gospel—is about God reconciling and restoring what was lost.

How does this fit with development and human flourishing? God's plan is to be present on this earth through the Holy Spirit in those who follow him. Empowered by the Holy Spirit, his followers are to bring healing, justice, truth, goodness, and beauty to the world. This presence and empowering of God in us is only fully possible through the saving work of Christ.

This is how the gospel and development connect!

In the evangelical church on a typical Sunday, we sing much about how Christ's atonement brings us grace, forgiveness, and freedom from the guilt and shame of sin and about how it restores our relationship with God and gives us the promise of eternal life with him. We sing about the Holy Spirit and ask him to be present with and help us. However there are very few songs about how the gospel restores us to our God-given vocation on this earth—to reflect God's nature and to bring restoration and flourishing to the world around us. We need to write some more songs!

PART 2

God's Design at Creation for Flourishing

In Genesis 1 and 2, we see God's design for how mankind is to live and function—our vocation. Adam and Eve were made to flourish and to bring flourishing to the world around them. This design was God's glory. When they sinned this vocation was broken and distorted, but God's intention did not change. It remained the same.

In this section, we will look at six essential components of God's remarkable design for all mankind. They address the basic worldview questions about life: Is there a spiritual reality? If so, what is it? What does it mean to be human? What is our relationship to the natural world? What is our purpose? Why are we here? I believe these are the foundational building blocks of a flourishing life and society.

1. Made to Flourish

As we all experience sooner or later, life is filled with hardship. A good friend is diagnosed with brain cancer. A family faces unemployment. A business owner loses one too many sales. A community fights a life-threatening virus. A nation struggles with rampant corruption and poverty. These kinds of things are par for the course.

And yet, somehow, we sense that this is not how life is supposed to be. Something is wrong. We not only *want* life to be better, we think it *should* be better. Why?

Looking at the book of Genesis, we discover that we have been created to flourish. To flourish means to grow well and thrive. It speaks of vigorous growth, productivity, and bearing fruit. A flourishing plant is full of rich color, beautiful flowers, wonderful fragrance, and delicious fruit.

Human flourishing, in turn, concerns how individuals and communities can develop and live in the most healthy and productive ways. It is not limited to economic gain and material progress. God's intent for flourishing covers every part of life—work, rest, entertainment, relationships, marriage, sex, family, church, food, hobbies, and vacations. Nothing is excluded. Everything is part of God's intent for flourishing and, therefore, is sacred.

In its fullest sense, the word *flourishing* is akin to the Hebrew word *shalom*. Translated *peace* in the Old Testament, *shalom* occurs more than 250 times. The general meaning of the root word is *of entering into a state of wholeness and unity, a restored relationship*. It also conveys a wide range of nuances: fulfillment, completion, maturity, soundness, wholeness, harmony, tranquility, security, well-being, welfare, friendship, agreement, success, and prosperity.[1]

Psalm 1 describes flourishing in this way: "He is like a tree planted by streams of water that yields its fruit in its season, and its leaf does not wither. In all that he does, he prospers." This is stated again in Jeremiah 17:8: "They will be like a tree planted by the water that sends out its roots by the stream. It does not fear when heat comes; its leaves are always green. It has no worries in a year of drought and never fails to bear fruit."

As these verses indicate, flourishing is not the same as avoiding difficulty. Helen Keller was blind and deaf, yet by her own account she lived a full and fruitful life. George Washington Carver was born into slavery, became an orphan at a young age, and faced prejudice and discrimination that delayed and almost halted his education. Yet he flourished, becoming one of the world's most productive scientists.

One of my heroes is Raquel. She lives in a poor community outside of Lima, Peru. Raquel worked all her life as a housekeeper, earning very low pay. Yet today all her children are educated, successful adults and her home is one of the nicest in the neighborhood. With all her difficulties, how did this happen?

---

1   Efraim Goldstein, "A Study on Biblical Concepts of Peace in the Old and New Testaments" (Jews for Jesus, 1997), https://jewsforjesus.org/publications/newsletter/december-1997/studyonbiblical.

God made us to flourish—to grow and prosper—to live *shalom*! He desires this blessed state for us, and he desires it for the world.

In Genesis 1 God creates the world and everything in it. He makes the land to *produce* vegetation, plants, and trees that *bear fruit* and *multiply* or *increase*. Creating fish, birds, and land animals, God blesses them and says, "*Be fruitful and increase* in number and *fill* the seas and the earth" (emphasis added). This opening chapter of the Bible shows how God has wired growth and fruitfulness right into creation.

God creates his world to be a really good place. After each act of creation, God steps back and sees that *it is good*. We read, "God called the dry ground 'land,' and the gathered waters he called 'seas.' And God saw that it was *good*."[2] On the sixth day, "God saw all that he had made, and it was *very good*."[3] "The Lord God made all kinds of trees grow out of the ground—trees that were *pleasing to the eye* and *good* for food."[4]

God makes the world a good place and then commands human beings to make it *even better*. Before the fall, before any hint of sin and brokenness enters the world, God gives mankind an overarching reason for being here—a mission to carry out, a task to do.

In Genesis 1:27 God makes male and female in his image and commands them to be fruitful, increase in numbers, fill the earth, and rule over it. In Genesis 2:15 we see that "The Lord God took the man and put him in the Garden of Eden to work it and take care of it." Adam and Eve were to work the garden and make it even more fruitful.

---

2   Genesis 1:10 (NIV).
3   Genesis 1:31.
4   Genesis 2:9.

God intended for Adam and Eve to improve the good things he had given them. They were to use their ingenuity and effort to develop every aspect of life and improve its function. Some theologians call this first commandment the creation mandate or the cultural mandate, while others call it the cultural commission in order to connect it with the Great Commission. We are called to create culture—language, food, government, schools, systems—everything that constitutes the societies and communities in which we live.

In Genesis 3 Adam and Eve disobey God, allowing sin to enter the world. While sin is a destructive force that affects everything, it does not change God's intention for flourishing and goodness in this world. God does not decide, even at this point, that flourishing and goodness only apply to the spiritual realm.

No, he remains committed to his creation and the people he placed here. God did not create the world and life to be *very good* in Genesis 1 and 2 only to change his mind when sin entered the picture in Genesis 3. God did not change his purpose for mankind. He did not stop caring deeply about all dimensions of human life, both here on earth and eternally.

God's response throughout the Old Testament and into the New is to call his people back to a place of flourishing and goodness in this life as he designed it. In Jeremiah 31 God's promise to Israel for restoration and healing is earthly and tangible—it is not purely spiritual. He promises his people they will be planting vineyards and enjoying the fruit. They will be rejoicing in the bounty of grain, new wine and olive oil, flocks and herds.

We see this intention fully expressed in Jesus as he heals the sick and the lame, feeds the 5,000, helps fishermen with their catch, gives sight to blind, restores the outcast, and even turns water into good wine at a wedding.

Colossians 1 tells us that Christ died to reconcile all things in heaven and on earth. "All things" includes not just human souls but the physical world as well. God intends to renew the whole of creation. N. T. Wright says[5] that this is why the literal resurrection of Jesus to a new physical body is such a big deal. God cares about the physical earth and physical bodies and the things of everyday life. He made us in his image to care the same.

This understanding of Genesis 1 and 2 is important, because it gives our lives direction and purpose. The fall of mankind and its effects are very real. The world is broken; life is indeed difficult. But the larger reality is that God made us and all of creation to flourish, and he gave us the privilege and responsibility to work toward this…even after the fall.

Standing in contrast to this grand purpose are the competing worldviews of materialism and those worldviews that lead to fatalism.

Materialism says that we can change things, but "things" are all we have. It holds that:

- This world is all there is.
- There is no Creator God or relationship with him.
- There are no more days other than those we have in this life.
- There is no purpose beyond the meaning we attach to or derive from our things or life itself.

Fatalism says we can ultimately do nothing to change our lives and the world for good. Those in the grip of animistic religions

---

5   N. T. Wright, *Surprised by Hope: Rethinking Heaven, the Resurrection, and the Mission of the Church* (New York: HarperOne, 2008).

hold that the gods of this world control and shape the events of life. Others believe that actions and events are determined by an impersonal fate or providential destiny.

A man in Rwanda with a severe eye problem visited an ophthalmologist. The doctor treated his eye, which began healing nicely. But midway through the treatment, before the eye could fully heal, the man returned to his village. Why? He said he needed a witch doctor to address the curse that had caused the ailment.

Chris Ampadu of Ghana, who teaches churches in West Africa, says that this kind of fatalism limits development in Africa. He says it comes from an animistic worldview that causes people to believe they have no real control over their lives.[6]

In some respects, dispensational eschatology arising from an incomplete view of the Christian faith encouraged fatalistic thinking in Western churches.

In dispensational theology the "new heaven and new earth" are an entirely separate place beyond this world, which is ultimately doomed. From this perspective I understood that God cares only about the soul of mankind...and that the primary reason Jesus restored things and healed people was to show God's love and to prove that he was God so that they would believe in him. Similarly, we are to show God's love so that others will respond to the message of salvation and go to heaven when they die.

However, Isaiah 66:22 reflects the expectation of the Jewish hope that God would one day come and renew the heavens and the earth. Revelation 21 tells us that the new heaven comes when Christ returns to dwell with us, and heaven and earth become one. The new earth is *this* earth, renewed. Yes, the world will be

---

6   Chris Ampadu, interview (2014), https://vimeo.com/96033883.

"shaken" and "burned" and thereby cleansed of sin and unrighteousness, but it will not be completely destroyed.

While the fall of mankind and its effects in Genesis 3 are devastatingly real, it seems clear from the rest of Scripture that God's intention at creation in Genesis 1 and 2 is unchanged and relates to the here and now. He desires good/flourishing for mankind and creation and has appointed to us the responsibility and privilege to carry this out.

All of this may sound abstract and academic, but truly grasping this biblical perspective has major implications for how we live. Some Christians in war-torn South Sudan put it like this:

Adili: "We still have hope, no matter how the situation looks."

Joseph: "We are charged to take care of the whole of creation."

Jok: "I had the thought that South Sudan was cursed, but now I know different. God has [blessed] and will bless South Sudan."

God desires flourishing for all people and all of creation just as he did at creation, despite the brokenness of fallen humanity. Knowing we are made to flourish gives us purpose, vision, and motivation for our daily lives.

2. Made to Know God

Flourishing lives, families, businesses, and communities do not just fall from the sky. They come not from luck, having the right geography, or access to natural resources.

Just as a tree requires certain elements in order to grow and thrive, certain principles undergird all human flourishing. As the Creator of all things, God knows what these principles are. He set them in place at creation and knows exactly how every area of life can best function and thrive.

Our ability to flourish begins with knowing the One who designed us to flourish and who is indeed the source of all flourishing. This is our starting point. "In the beginning, God..."

Who is this God who created the stage upon which each of us lives and dies? What is he like? What is his character like? Who are we in relationship to him? Why did he put us here and make us as we are? These are the first questions all religions and philosophies seek to answer—from atheism to Taoism.

Again the Bible says, "In the beginning, God created the heavens and the earth." God created everything. God gives life to and sustains everything. We live under the care and authority of the Creator God. Why then does so much sin and sadness persist in our world? The answer: We have rebelled against God and his design. Romans 1 reveals that a person or society that denies this first reality is on a path of increasing delusion, brokenness, and dissipation.

The predominant creation story in the West today is that life began entirely on its own from nonliving matter and developed through random mutation and natural selection. However, as scientists continue to learn more and more about living matter, this theory becomes a less and less sufficient explanation.[1]

In Genesis 1 and 2, Adam and Eve knew no such confusion. They knew God firsthand as Creator of the world they enjoyed. They knew him as the one who had formed and given them life, as the source and sustainer of all life, and as the wisdom and power behind everything they experienced.

In Acts 14:15 Paul urges the people of Lystra to turn from worthless things and know this living God: "We are bringing you good news, telling you to turn from these worthless things to the living God, who made the heavens and the earth and the sea and everything in them." And who is this living God?

The first prayer I remember learning as a child started with the words "God is great, God is good." The first Bible song I remember was "Jesus Loves Me."

It sounds simple, but if we had to boil down *knowing God* into three ideas, I think these three from my childhood—God's greatness, goodness, and love—work quite well.

God is great. God is the greatest in wisdom, knowledge, power, and authority. Everything else we consider great and powerful is a mere flicker in comparison. We live all of life before a great God.

God is good. Everything he is and does issues from a place of total goodness. Even his anger, wrath, and judgment of sin ultimately come from this goodness. All that is good comes from

---

1   "Intelligent Design FAQs & Primers,"
     http://www.ideacenter.org/resources/faq.php.

God. Beauty, wherever we find it, displays this goodness. If something is truly good, its source is God. We live our lives before the face of a *good* God.

God is love. God's determination for people and for his creation is always and only for good. This is what love is.

God is totally unique in his greatness, goodness, and love—God is holy.

I said three things but would add a fourth. That is, God is a *mystery.* All too often we look at the above three characteristics and say, like Job and his friends, that if God is great and God is good and God is love, then...He should do _____. But there are some questions about God that we cannot answer. I am reminded of Deuteronomy 29:29, which says, "The secret things belong to the Lord our God, but the things that are revealed belong to us and to our children forever, that we may do all the words of this law." Because of our finiteness, God is a mystery—there are things about him and his ways that we will never understand. Yet God is also knowable. Through his creation we can see his nature—his greatness, goodness, and love. God is revealed to us and desires to relate to us, but he will always be beyond our full comprehension.

This is the God we can know—truly, but not exhaustively.[2]

Adam and Eve walked and talked with God, free from shame and self-consciousness. Appointed by him to rule over all creation, they knew they were blessed by him. They knew how they belonged and how they fit in. The result was freedom and self-governance, security and confidence, awe and gratitude—in a word, *flourishing.*

In a speech given in 1645, John Winthrop, deputy governor of Massachusetts, said, "Liberty is the proper end and object of

---

2   R. C. Sproul, "Divine Incomprehensibility" (Ligonier Ministries), http://www.ligonier.org/learn/articles/divine-incomprehensibility/.

authority and cannot subsist without it."[3] Our natural inclination is to want to live free of authority, but the reality is we need it. Societies need the authority of rules and laws. Students need the authority of teachers. Workers need supervisors. Teams need team leaders. Bosses need boards. Countries need constitutions. Even kings derive their right to rule from a higher power or from the will of God. John Winthrop was right. We all need authority, and the liberty and goodness we desire cannot subsist without it.

The Bible says there is one supreme cosmic authority and that this authority is good.

In contrast to this, Psalm 14:1 says, "The fool says in his heart, 'There is no God.' They are corrupt, they do abominable deeds; there is none who does good."

God's design for human flourishing and development begins with knowing him, the divine author of it all. We are made to know the God who created the heavens and the earth—to know him as Creator and King, Father and Friend. God is the great designer and brilliant orchestrator of all of life, and he rules over it in perfect goodness.

In Genesis 3 we fell from knowing this God as we should. Through the cross of Christ, we are saved to know him anew and to stand in the secure place of daughter and son.

---

3   John Winthrop, "On Liberty" (1645),
    http://www.constitution.org/bcp/winthlib.htm.

3. Made in the Image of God

In the last chapter, we looked at the wonderful fact that people have been made to know God. Yet how is it even possible for finite and fallen human beings to know the infinite and infinitely good God, who created and sustains everything? In the Old Testament, Job, lamenting his plight, gave voice to the natural distance that we often feel from our Creator: "Why do you hide your face and consider me your enemy" (Job 13:24)?

However, the same Bible that shows followers of God struggling to understand their Creator also reveals him as eager to walk with us and teach us his ways. What makes this kind of relationship possible? The answer is found in the first chapter in the Bible: "So God created mankind in his own image, in the image of God he created them; male and female he created them" (Gen. 1:27).

This verse provides *the basis* for the intrinsic equal value and dignity of *every* person. All of us—male and female, young and old, rich and poor, able-bodied or disabled, brilliant or mentally challenged, intellectually or practically gifted—are made in the image of God. There are no exceptions. This is why we can relate to God. This is also why we have the potential to bring about the flourishing that he desires.

The implications of this truth are profound and multiple. Without this exalted view of humanity, we possess no real basis for believing in the intrinsic dignity and equal value of all human beings. This foundation for human dignity is found in no other religion or philosophy. If we are not all created in the image of God, male and female, we have no sustainable rationale for human equality.

For example, William Sumner, an Episcopal priest who subsequently abandoned his faith in Christ, said, "A man has no more right to life than a rattlesnake; he has no more right to liberty than any wild beast; his right to pursuit of happiness is nothing but a license to maintain the struggle for existence."[1]

Even the Universal Declaration of Human Rights, ratified by the United Nations in 1948, does not provide a sure foundation for human dignity and equality. It was based ultimately on the opinion of men and women and ratified by many (but not all) nations. We must remember that human opinions and the votes of nations can change...and often do.

By contrast the Bible, which is the unchanging word of God, tells us that *all* people are made in the image of God, the *imago Dei*. Thus the Bible provides the only foundation for our belief in inherent human dignity and universal human rights.

Denying this truth that we are made in the image of God is the single greatest cause of misery and poverty on this planet. In the absence of this truth, we have countless forms of harm and injustice every day in all countries and among all peoples:

- Slavery
- Infanticide/abortion

---

1   William Graham Sumner and Albert Galloway Keller, *Earth-hunger and Other Essays* (New Haven, Conn.: Yale University Press, 1913), 234.

- Genocide
- Gendercide
- Spousal abuse
- Sexual abuse
- Child abuse
- Racism
- Tribalism
- Discrimination
- Narcissism
- Self-hatred

In contrast to all this, the Bible teaches that every person bears the image of God equally. No one is "less made" in the likeness of God.

It is true that we differ from each other in many ways. We differ in age, sex, race, height, weight, nationality, physical strength, tribal group, education, mental ability, status, wealth, religion—the list can go on and on. Yet because we are all made in the likeness and image of God, every one of us, from conception to death, shares the same intrinsic dignity and value in the sight of God.

Creation stories matter. A church leader from another country told me how his tribe's creation story actually positioned a neighboring tribe as subhuman. He recognized that this myth was one of the deep contributing roots to the long-standing enmity between their two tribes.

When sin entered the world, it distorted everything—especially our understanding of ourselves as made in the image of God. Immediately, Adam blames Eve for *his* disobedience. Enmity grows between them. Cain becomes jealous and angry with Abel and kills him. All of the evils listed above had begun.

In Jesus's day, all kinds of divisions existed between groups that claimed superiority over one another. There were Romans over non-Romans, Jews over Gentiles, men over women, free over slave, adult over child, healthy over sick, and rich over poor.

Yet Jesus saw every person as a full image-bearer of God and treated each accordingly, with dignity and value. He welcomed children. He included women in his group of close friends. He touched badly deformed lepers. He dined with corrupt tax collectors and even visited their homes. In a story about being a good neighbor, he recast a despised Samaritan as the good neighbor.

Jesus did *not* see people as superior or inferior. He saw people of all shapes and sizes and statuses as image-bearers—equal in intrinsic dignity and worth. He also saw all people equal in their fallen condition. John 2:24 says that Jesus did not entrust himself to people because he knew human nature. Part of our human commonality is that we all fall short of God's glory—his divine design. As Aleksandr Solzhenitsyn so famously said, "The line separating good and evil passes not through states, nor between classes, nor between political parties either—but right through every human heart."[2]

Who are we to judge others as superior or inferior, when the God of the universe does not? Still, in our arrogance and ignorance, we do this quite naturally. We all assign superiority or inferiority in reference to ourselves and others. This is tragic.

I met a man recently whose twenty-seven-year-old son has severe autism. The son can only groan and squeal—he cannot speak. He will never go to school or hold a job. Yet his dad does not see him as a victim or helpless. He sees him as an image-bearer

---

2 Aleksandr Solzhenitsyn, *The Gulag Archipelago Abridged: An Experiment in Literary Investigation* (New York: Harper Perennial Modern Classics, 2007), 312.

with infinite worth in the sight of God…and with a profound purpose. The father's understanding of this truth about his son has produced an unexpectedly beautiful degree of flourishing that would humble the proudest person.

When you look at someone, what do you see first? Do you see status, appearance, education, wealth, religion, or position? Based on this, do you perceive this person as either inferior or superior to you? Or do you immediately see him or her as an image-bearer of God, equal in dignity and value to you and all others? Do you see this person as loved by God?

Another important reality is that each person is made wonderfully unique. There are more than seven billion of us living here on planet Earth today and no two of us are alike. I am an identical twin and yet my brother and I are quite different. He knows how to design and build oil drilling rigs. I know relief and development work. He thinks about engineering problems. I think about worldview challenges. He likes to sing. I like to read. He is five feet, ten inches tall. I am five feet, ten and three-quarters.

God made every person on this planet unique in so many ways. Psalm 139:13–16 says, "For you formed my inward parts; you knitted me together in my mother's womb. I praise you, for I am fearfully and wonderfully made. Wonderful are your works; my soul knows it very well. My frame was not hidden from you, when I was being made in secret, intricately woven in the depths of the earth. Your eyes saw my unformed substance; in your book were written, every one of them, the days that were formed for me, when as yet there was none of them."

There is no such thing as an "ordinary person." We are *all* extraordinary. Each of us is an original. Every person is made unique.

Why is this truth vital to the flourishing of an individual, a community, or a nation?

Saint Thomas Aquinas (1225–1274) believed that God made each person unique in order to reflect him in a way no one else can. Aquinas wrote, "It would take an infinite number of human beings to mirror back the infinite facets of God. Each person reflects only a small—but beautiful—part of the whole."[3]

Our uniqueness suggests that each of us has a special role to play on this earth. No other person occupies your specific time and place in world history. No one else possesses your specific relationships, personality, experiences, and mix of abilities. Your role and place are vital. No one can fill your shoes and take your spot in God's plan for his world and the people in it.

The wealth of a community is the sum value of each of its citizens. The nation of Singapore understands this better than most. While this tiny land mass—the most densely populated country in the world—has few natural resources and must import its drinking water from nearby Malaysia, in 2012 it was the third-most prosperous country in the world per capita. How can this be?

Singaporean society values the potential of *all* of its citizens, not just a select few. Thus Singapore's education system ranks among the world's best. The nation expects everyone to develop to his or her fullest potential and contribute for the benefit of all. No one is exempt.

Or consider South Korea. In the mid-1950s, over half of the population was living in absolute poverty. By the mid-1990s, however, the poverty rate had plunged to only 3.4 percent. South Korea's zeal for the development of its people through education and training is legendary. An amazing 97 percent of its young

---

3 Novak, Michael, *Three in One: Essays on Democratic Capitalism, 1976-2000* (Lanham, Maryland: Rowman & Littlefield, 2001), 247.

people achieve a secondary school diploma, 65 percent a postsecondary diploma.

A nation's most valuable resource is not its geographic location, its oil, its land, or even its history. A nation's most valuable resource is its people. A community or nation that wants to develop well will create an environment and an expectation that encourages and supports each individual citizen to develop and apply themselves to their fullest potential.

In Luke 2:52 we read that Jesus "grew in wisdom and stature and in favor with God and man." This growth comes from within. Others cannot "grow" us. They may help us in this process, but we are called by God to grow (steward) the life he has given us and use it for good.

Jesus's story of the three stewards in Matthew 25:14–30 makes this point well. In this parable a very wealthy man is about to go on a long trip. He calls his three servants together and tells them he is leaving them in charge of all of his wealth before dividing and distributing it to them.

To the first servant, he gives five talents. To the second, he gives two. To the third, he gives one. The first takes the five talents and earns five more. The second also invests his two talents wisely and earns two more. The third servant, however, takes his single talent and buries it.

When the master returns, he is very pleased when the first two servants tell him they have doubled his money, and he gives them even more. However, he is angry with the third, who, being afraid, has buried the money for safekeeping. The master then takes the talent from him and gives it to the one who has ten talents.

There are several lessons here for us. First, as in real life, there are no guarantees. To invest is to risk. Yet the faithful stewards invest what they are entrusted with, get a good return, and are rewarded.

Second, the master gives each steward a different amount to invest but expects them all to invest well. In our own lives, we all have differing abilities and resources, but God gives each of us equal responsibility to invest well whatever we've been given.

Third, the story reminds us that we are stewards. A steward is one who administers for "best use" the property and resources entrusted to him or her by another.

As the Creator, God owns everything and entrusts his possessions to us. Each of us has been entrusted by God with a life, a mind, abilities, and resources. We are to develop these gifts and put them to "best use" to reflect the One whose image we bear and to fulfill his purposes for this world. We should encourage and help one another do the same.

My friend Geeta in New Delhi understands this perspective on stewardship. She founded and directs an education program for children with learning challenges. The prevailing view in her community says that these children are reaping the karma of their past life and should not be helped.

Geeta, however, views every person as affected by the fall of mankind in one way or another. She also sees each of these children as made in the image of God, with a special reflection of God to show the world and a unique contribution to make to humanity. The lives of these children are dramatically different as a result of her vision and persistence!

God made every human life in his image, so we are special. Each human life is of equal value and worth in the sight of God and a unique reflection of him. Each is made to reflect God to all creation. Each of us has a role to play, a gift to offer, and a contribution to make on this earth. As John Adams said, "To act well your part, there all the honor lies."[4]

Understanding this vital truth and living it out is the path to flourishing for an individual, a community, and a nation.

It begins with every person developing and stewarding what they have been given by God—their body, mind, imagination, abilities, and opportunities.

> "And Jesus kept increasing in wisdom and in stature,
> and in favor with God and men."
>
> *– Luke 2:52 (AMP)*

---

4   David McCullough, *John Adams* (Simon & Schuster, 2002), 171.

4. Made to Create

In the Bible's opening chapter, we see God creating the universe and mankind. To create is to transcend what is. God imagines what ought to be, and he creates it. God makes man and woman in his image and immediately commands them to continue the work that he has begun.

"Then God said, *'Let us make man in our image, after our likeness. And let them have dominion over* the fish of the sea and over the birds of the heavens and over the livestock *and over all the earth* and over every creeping thing that creeps on the earth'...*And God blessed them.* And God said to them, 'Be fruitful and multiply and *fill the earth and subdue it,* and *have dominion* over the fish of the sea and over the birds of the heavens and over every living thing that moves on the earth'" (Gen. 1:26, 28; emphasis added). The NIV reads, "Let us make mankind in our image, in our likeness, *so that* they may *rule over...*" (emphasis added).

Genesis 2:15 follows: "The Lord God took the man and put him in the garden of Eden to *work it* [cultivate/dress] and *keep it* [take care of, steward, maintain" (emphasis added).

God's first command in the Bible was not the Ten Commandments, the Great Commandment, or the Great Commission. It was the command to *work*—to rule over—the earth. My colleague Darrow Miller says that God made the world perfect, but he did not make it complete. He gave the job of completing it to the ones he made in his likeness—his image-bearers.

God both creates and rules. Because we are made in his image, we are made to create and to rule. We are to have dominion over creation and all of life. This is what it means to be human. Psalm 8:5–8 (NIV) says, "You have made them a little lower than the angels and crowned them with glory and honor. You made them rulers over the works of your hands; you put everything under their feet: all flocks and herds, and the animals of the wild, the birds in the sky, and the fish in the sea, all that swim the paths of the seas."

No other religion or worldview offers such a high view of human beings.

Theologians often refer to this first command as the cultural mandate. We are to take what God has provided and create with it—to create all that makes up our life on earth, that is, to create culture.

In short, we are to take what God has given us and make something with it. We are to make the world a better place.

Nancy Pearcey, in her book *Total Truth*, explains why it's called the cultural mandate.

> The first phrase, 'be fruitful and multiply,' means to develop the social world: build families, churches, schools, cities, governments, laws. The second phrase, 'subdue the earth,' means to harness the natural world: plant crops, build bridges, design computers, and compose music. This passage is sometimes called the cultural mandate

because it tells us that our original purpose was to create cultures, build civilizations—nothing less.[1]

One of the big lies in our world is that work is a curse. Consequently, the really fortunate person is the one who does not have to work. Yet throughout Scripture we see that God himself works (Gen. 1:1, 31; John 5:17). We also see that before sin and suffering entered the world, God created work and gave us work to do. Work, as given by God, is not a curse. It carries dignity and divine purpose.

The command to rule over the earth—to make the world a better place, to make life function well—is universal and transcends culture. It applies to everyone, everywhere, at all times. It applies to the rich, the poor, the weak, the strong, the young, and the old. It covers every area of life: farming, accounting, software development, government, education, marriage, family, cooking, and even entertainment. We are to take what God has given us and create good in all these spheres.

God not only *commanded* us to govern and create, he *wired* us to do so. God has put into each of us an appreciation for beauty and order and a desire to create. Give a child a pencil and paper, and she will immediately begin to draw something. We see an empty room and envision a way to fill it—add a chair here, hang a picture there, install a light over there. We see a misspelled word or an addition error, and we want to correct it. We clean. We find a stain on a shirt and apply soap and water to remove it. We see lint on our coat, and we flick it away. We continually seek to improve and add efficiency.

---

1   Nancy Pearcey, *Total Truth: Liberating Christianity from Its Cultural Captivity* (Wheaton: Crossway, 2008), 47.

We are made by God to create—to improve, fix, heal, organize, restore, add, beautify—to make life and the world better.

All this seems natural and obvious, but do we recognize it as the fundamental first purpose God gave us when he put us on this earth? Do we see this as a sacred task? Are we doing it well? Are we taking all that God has entrusted to us and creating what is good and beautiful—for others, for our families, and for ourselves?

Adam did not waste any time but went right to work. In Genesis 2:19–20 he takes on the task of creating names for all the animals. That was no small task when you consider Adam was new with language and there were thousands of unnamed animals!

We see an example of the effects of this command to create in Revelation 21. Genesis 2 lists raw materials such as gold, resin, and onyx, and in Revelation 21 we see these same materials refined and incorporated into the foundations and walls of the new Jerusalem. Somebody mined these minerals and used them as building materials. I find this fascinating.

We All Have Resources

One of Satan's biggest deceptions is to convince us that that we have no resources. We often feel we have so little to work with in comparison with others. But however much or little we have, like the faithful stewards, we are called to recognize, develop, and apply the resources God has given us.

Even the poorest person on earth has the single greatest resource possible—a human mind and imagination. Most everything you have and enjoy in life is the result of someone developing and using his or her mind. God puts oil into the ground, but it is the human imagination that creates plastic and artificial hips from that oil. God puts sand on the seashore, but it is the human mind that fashions it into silicone chips that power computers and smartphones. God makes wheat, but the creative human mind makes croissants.

William Kamkwamba, age 14, lived in poverty in a village in Malawi. During a severe famine, William had to drop out of school, but he didn't drop out from learning.[2] He checked out several books on electricity at the village library, and using cast-off materials William built an electricity-generating windmill at his house. When others learned of his amazing accomplishment, he gave a TEDx Talk and eventually received a scholarship to study engineering at a South African university.[3]

From the son of the poor farmer to the daughter of the wealthy banker, all of us have the incredible resource of the mind and the heart to use it well. The challenge is to develop these gifts.

The Fall Did Not Change Our Task

As I have said, the fall of mankind did not nullify God's command to fill and govern the earth. Sin made fulfilling this task much more difficult, but God still wants us to take what he provides and make the world a better place.

What does obedience to this command look like in a fallen world? It looks like my friend doing accurate accounting for his clients. It looks like the mom in rural Uganda using her small savings to buy a mosquito net to place over her child's bed. It looks like our mayor and city manager making decisions to improve the function and livability of our city. It looks like the research scientist in our church who is working on a cure for cancer. It looks like my

---

2   William Kamkwamba and Bryan Mealer, *The Boy Who Harnessed the Wind* (New York: Harper Collins, 2010).

3   See https://www.ted.com/participate/organize-a-local-tedx-event/tedx-organizer-guide/speakers-program/what-is-a-tedx-talk.

neighbor putting up amazing Christmas lights. It looks like the maintenance guy in our complex fixing and restoring what breaks.

Many Christians don't see this kind of work as particularly "Christian." Yet in bringing good to this world and blessing others, they are aligning themselves with God's divine purpose. The flourishing of an individual life and a nation hinges on how well people work and create good—how well they fulfill the first commandment.

My colleague Scott Allen sums it up this way:

> People are not fundamentally consumers of resources but creators of resources. God has blessed every human being with talents, gifts, and abilities. He expects us to use these to expand the garden, to leave this magnificent world better than we found it. More fruitful, more prosperous. Theologian James Smith puts it like this. He said, "When God called creation into being, he announced that it's very good. He doesn't announce that it's finished. Creation doesn't come into existence ready-made with schools and art museums and farms. All of those are begging to be unpacked. The riches and the potential of God's good creation are entrusted to his image-bearers. That is our calling and our commission."[4] The cultural mandate is your job description. It's never been rescinded. We are to use our hands, our minds, our talents, our resources, to make this world better. That's why we are here. That's our purpose in life.[5]

We are made to create. God's creative work in Genesis 1 and 2 was perfect but not complete. He delegated the completion of the

---

4   James K. A. Smith, *Letters for a Young Calvinist: An Invitation to the Reformed Tradition* (Grand Rapids: Brazos Press, 2010), 109.

5   Scott Allen, "Lesson 6: The Great Commission and the Cultural Commission" (2015), www.coramdeo.com.

task to every person. God told us to rule over and develop the world, to create human society and culture, and to bring about the full flourishing of life as he intended—in short, to make life better. In Genesis 3 this task became distorted and made a thousand times more difficult by sin. Yet God saves us through Christ to do this task anew—each one of us with a unique role to play.

5. Made to Benefit One Another

God's design for human flourishing is found in his commands. The Ten Commandments[1] give us a divinely inspired list of principles for living a good life and creating a well-functioning community and nation. The five books of Moses add hundreds more commandments to the list. In the New Testament, Jesus boils them all down to the Great Commandment: Love God, and love your neighbor.

In Matthew 22:36–40 we read, "'Teacher, which is the great commandment in the Law?" And [Jesus] said to him, 'You shall love the Lord your God with all your heart and with all your soul and with all your mind. This is the great and first commandment. And a second is like it: You shall love your neighbor as yourself. On these two commandments depend all the Law and the Prophets.'"

The Apostle Paul picks up this principle in Galatians 5:14, where we read, "For the entire law is fulfilled in keeping this one command: 'Love your neighbor as yourself'"; and in Romans 13:8 and 10 it says, "the one who loves another has fulfilled the law" and "Love does no wrong to a neighbor; therefore, love is the fulfilling of the law."

---

1   Exodus 20:1–17.

Bob Moffitt refers to this great commandment as the "irreducible minimum" of God's requirements.[2] It is the summation of all the virtues. Human flourishing hinges on loving your neighbor.

What does it mean to love your neighbor?

We typically associate love with some sense of affection and warmth for another person. Or we frame "loving your neighbor" as individual acts of kindness…as going out of our way to do something especially kind for another. While these notions are not wrong in themselves, the concept is much bigger.

In simplest terms, to love your neighbor is to determine and do the highest good for the other person. In Latin *bene facere* means to "do good to" and is where we get the word "benefit." To love your neighbor is to benefit them. For example, plumbers love their neighbor by providing reliable piping for clean water and sanitation in a home. They may never see the homeowner, but their quality work contributes to the good of that person. In turn, the homeowner loves the plumber by giving a complete, on-time payment so the plumber can feed and provide for his family.

While this kind of thing sounds like a business transaction, at its heart this is a mutual exchange of benefit and good that reflects God's design for human flourishing. God actually set the world up to function this way.

Highly successful sports teams get this principle. They know that they must serve and maximize the roles and abilities of each member for the greater good. That is, they must love one another. I recently heard a coach interviewed after winning a national championship. When he was asked what he told his team before

---

2   Bob Moffitt, "What Is the Irreducible Minimum?" https://vimeo.com/89713159.

the big game, he said, "I just told them to go out there and love one another."

We can see this principle to love (benefit) one another already at work in Genesis 2:18: "It is not good for the man to be alone. I will make a helper suitable for him."

The word *helper* here is the Hebrew word *ezer*.[3] King David used this word in saying "God is my helper" (*ezer*). The *ezer* is one who provides help or ability that another lacks. Eve provided what Adam lacked, and vice versa. Adam and Eve were made to love, to do good to one another, to benefit each other.

Every one of us is lacking in some way. We need one another to survive and to develop. None of us would thrive if we lived alone on an island. What kind of life would you have without farmers, builders, electricians, doctors, nurses, mail carriers, teachers, and cooks? Consider how many people have served you throughout the day. You may think first of the obvious ones, such as the young man who hands you your coffee or the worker who collects the trash on your street. But don't forget the woman who built the chair you sit on and the man who harvested the cotton to make the cloth in your shirt.

While economies and societies are complex, at a basic level they are about people doing good things that benefit one another. When this principle is broken, you see diminished nations, communities, and families. You see poverty.

A common cause of societal failure is zero-sum thinking. That is, life and resources are seen like a pie. If someone gets more, another must get less. If one person gains, another must lose. But God's design for the world is *not* zero-sum. It is that flourishing

---

3 Strong's Concordance, http://biblehub.com/hebrew/5828.htm.

comes by people working, creating, and living in mutually beneficial ways—doing good for one another.

Individuals and communities flourish when people live to benefit one another. This "love your neighbor" principle undergirds the health and strength of marriage, family, business, and government. When it fails, these institutions fail.

What Is Good?

If loving your neighbor is to seek and do the highest good for them, the all-important question we must ask is, "What is *good*?" How we answer this question is critical to the flourishing of individuals and nations. Modern society says that people decide for *themselves* what is good, with the only restriction being that their decision does not harm another person. This approach falls short because one person's view of what is good invariably conflicts with another's. Like truth, good cannot be relative.

In his book *After Virtue,* philosopher Alasdair MacIntyre argues that you cannot know whether something is good or bad unless you know the purpose for which it was designed, that is, its *telos.*[4] He gives a watch as an example.

If you hammer a nail with a watch and the watch breaks, that doesn't make the watch bad or hammering a nail bad. It makes *using a watch to hammer a nail* bad. This is because the watch was not designed to hammer nails but to tell time. To know whether something is good or bad, you must know the purpose (*telos*) for which it was designed. The same applies to human beings and human behavior.

---

4   Alasdair MacIntyre, *After Virtue: A Study in Moral Theory*, Third Edition (South Bend, University of Notre Dame Press, 2007).

So who defines the *telos* of something, whether a watch, a hammer, or a human being? The answer is obvious. It is the *creator* of a watch or a hammer that defines its purpose. In the same way, *God* defines the *telos* for human beings and how we are designed to live and function best. Whatever aligns with and support this purpose and design we rightly call "good" (moral). Whatever does not align with or works against this purpose we rightly call "not good" (immoral). To know what is good for someone or something we have to know its purpose and design.

The prophet Isaiah wrote about the importance of discerning good correctly: "Woe to those who call evil good and good evil, who put darkness for light and light for darkness, who put bitter for sweet and sweet for bitter!"[5] In a similar vein, Jesus warned, "Your eye is the lamp of your body. When your vision is clear, your whole body also is full of light. But when it is poor, your body is full of darkness."[6] And the prophet Amos wrote: "You turn what is right into something bitter. You throw what is right and good down to the earth."[7]

Human flourishing hinges on people loving their neighbors well. Loving well hinges on knowing what is good. Knowing and doing what is good for people requires knowing the purpose for which they are designed and created.

Is your community or nation marked by a mind-set of people knowing and doing what's good for one another? Do you know what is truly good and best for others? Do you have the courage to pursue this, even if others don't define good the same way?

If so, you are on a path that leads to flourishing.

---

5   Isaiah 5:20.
6   Luke 11:34 (NIV).
7   Amos 5:7 (NLT).

Individuals and communities flourish when people live to benefit one another. This is how we were designed to live in Genesis 1. This vocation was distorted and broken by sin. Jesus died to restore it, to give us wisdom and power through his Spirit to fully love as God intends.

6. Made to Rest

In all my years working to help communities and their members, I never thought much about the principle of rest. It seemed obvious that everyone needs to take a break once in a while. Wherever I traveled and worked, people always took at least one day off from their regular jobs each week. What I didn't grasp was the difference between a restorative rest and a just-taking-a-break rest. I didn't make the important connection between rest, play, and entertainment. The difference is thriving or surviving.

Scripture and life itself tell us that rest is a key part of flourishing and thriving. To function well, everything needs to rest. God knew this and commanded it: "By the seventh day God had finished the work he had been doing; so on the seventh day he rested from all his work. Then God blessed the seventh day and made it holy, because on it he rested from all the work of creating that he had done" (Gen. 2:2–3). "Remember the Sabbath day, to keep it holy" (Exod. 20:8).

If we and our communities are to flourish, we must rest. The challenge for all of us is knowing when and how to rest well.

When I was twenty, I traveled with a musical ministry team for a year. On Sunday, "the day of rest," we were not allowed to play basketball or table tennis. We were told that "resting" was mandatory. Nonetheless, we were still obligated to set up sound and lighting equipment for our concerts on Sunday. Worse, we had to wear ties and jackets, even on the hottest days. Trust me, this arrangement felt like anything but good rest!

What Is Good Rest?

Mark Buchanan, in his book, *The Rest of God,* says that the rest God intends for us can be as simple as stopping and going in the opposite direction.[1] Buchanan suggests two things that constitute what he refers to as Sabbath's golden rule:

1. Cease from what is necessary.
2. Embrace that which gives life.[2]

Stop doing what you must. Shuck the "have-tos," and embrace the "get-tos." Stop working, and let the things you have made bless and serve you.

Buchanan says that one good way to do both is to play, which subverts necessity and utility. He says, "Play and Sabbath are joined at the hip, and sometimes we rest best when we play hardest."[3] If so our musical ministry team should have taken off our coats and ties on Sunday, played table tennis, and shot some baskets!

Rest has to be more than a mere escape from work or vacating the workplace (a vacation). Rest cannot be just the absence of work or the break we receive as a reward after completing a task. True rest adds richness and energy, which flow into the balance of one's life. It's like eating good food. We eat food for the satisfaction and pleasure of the moment, but food also gives us strength and energy

---

1   Mark Buchanan, *The Rest of God: Restoring Your Soul by Restoring Sabbath* (Nashville: Thomas Nelson, 2006).
2   Ibid, 129.
3   Ibid, 142 (emphasis in original).

for the hours ahead. The same is true of rest. It should renew, restore, revitalize, and rejuvenate us. It should recreate us, which is where we get the word "recreation!"

This command that leads to flourishing goes beyond personal rest. It includes land, companies, communities, and nations.

If you own a farm, are you treating the land in a way that it can be renewed? If you own a company or run an organization, do you remember your employees' need for rest and restoration? If you are a community, do you support days and events that bring rest and wholesome rejuvenation? If you are a nation, do you pass laws and policies that promote rest and renewal for people and resources?

Finally, if play and Sabbath are joined at the hip, entertainment is included because entertainment is a form of rest and play. In my country we spend a lot of time and money entertaining ourselves. Entertainment can be good or bad. It can be helpful or it can be harmful. How we entertain ourselves can restore us as individuals, families, and communities or it can distort, diminish, and even destroy us in mind, soul, and body. Choose wisely.

We are made to rest. We are made to step back from our work and, together with family and friends, recognize all the good that God has given us and enjoy it. We are made to cease working and remember that God is the ultimate provider of all that we have. We are made to give time to renew and refresh our mind, soul, and body as God designed.

To develop and flourish as God intended, individuals, families, communities, and nations must rest, play, and entertain themselves well.

****

God's glory is that all of creation function as he designed. The principles in this section are an essential part of his design. They are our vocation. We see that the more individuals and societies align with these principles, the more they flourish and prosper.

PART 3
The Power to Flourish

When Adam and Eve believed Satan's lie about God, sin entered the world and distorted every aspect of the life God had created. This includes our lives today.

Consider...

- We are made to flourish, but instead of security, hope, and confidence, many hearts and minds are gripped by fatalism—leading to passivity and dependency. *Life is too difficult. The challenges are too great. I cannot change. This is my fate. I don't have resources. Others must help me. Others must change. It all depends on the gods. I am trapped. I am cursed.*

- We are made to know God but often give him only minimal acknowledgement. We put our deepest trust in ourselves, in others, in things, and in ideas. The Bible calls these idols. This leads to a false sense of security, at best, and to insecurity and fear, at worst. We delude ourselves and live unaware of God and his kingship.

- We are all made in the image of God and thus are equal in intrinsic dignity and value in the sight of God, but we don't fully believe this. Our default is to judge others based on appearance, gender, tribe, race, income level, etc. and the result is discrimination, racism, and conflict. We use the same lens to judge ourselves and the result is a sense inadequacy and shame or false pride and arrogance.

- We are all made wonderfully unique as image-bearers, but we fail to fully value and steward our own and one another's uniqueness. Talents and abilities go unrecognized. Minds go undeveloped. Creativity goes untapped. We fail to hold each other accountable to develop and apply all the resources God has given us. We hesitate to help another succeed, fearful that their gain will be our loss.

- We are made to create—to rule over all creation, to take what God has given and make the world and life better. At best we fall short of this, and at worst we add to the world's brokenness. Instead of solving problems, we add to them. Instead of giving more than we take, we take more than we give. Instead of adding beauty and order, we cause disorder.

- We are made to love our neighbor—to seek and do the highest good for one another, to benefit one another. But we often put our own good first. Worse, we lose sight of what is actually good for others (their divine design), or we lack the courage to promote what is good when faced with resistance.

- We are made to rest amid our work and to enjoy the fruits of our labor. But the reality is we do not know how to rest and play well. Instead of enjoying rest and entertainment that nurtures and builds the human spirit, we choose that which diminishes and dissipates mind, soul, and body.

Sin entered God's world and distorted every aspect of life. Yet God's will for mankind and creation in Genesis 1 and 2 did not change. We are still called to flourish and bring flourishing to the world. Is it possible? We see these principles fully expressed in the life of Jesus.

- Jesus flourished.
- Jesus knew God, his Father.
- Jesus treated every person as a full image-bearer, equal in intrinsic dignity and loved by him—child and adult, poor and rich, female and male, sick and healthy, Gentile and Jew, tax collector and synagogue leader, soldier and civilian, slave and ruler. This was astonishing in a world that drew dividing lines and ascribed value and dignity to some but not to others. Jesus consistently valued individuals in their uniqueness and called them to develop and live as God had created them to live.
- Jesus took the cultural mandate seriously. He ruled over creation and made things better. Jesus did this through his work. As a carpenter he built things.[1] During his three-year traveling ministry, he calmed the storm, helped his disciples catch fish, created wedding wine from water, gave sight to the blind, healed lepers, restored the legs of a crippled man, and raised people from the dead.
- Jesus loved his neighbor. He understood God's design for people and responded to what he knew to be the highest good for them. Jesus lived to benefit others to the ultimate end—the cross.

---

1   Mark 6:3.

- Jesus rested. He honored the Sabbath, attended weddings, ate with his disciples, spent time alone, and took time to rejuvenate.[2]

Jesus fully lived out God's intentions on this earth. In doing so he flourished and brought flourishing like no one else.

Jesus calls us to do the same—and even more so. "Whoever believes in me will do the works I have been doing, and they will do even greater things than these, because I am going to the Father."[3] And he said we are to do these things perfectly "as our heavenly Father is perfect."[4]

Yet even when we know what to do and want to do it, we lack the power and ability. Our situation is like that of the Apostle Paul who wrote, "For I have the desire to do what is right, but not the ability to carry it out. For I do not do the good I want, but the evil I do not want is what I keep on doing."[5] "Who can set me free from my sinful, old self?"[6]

This is the human predicament. It is the world's predicament. God created us for a grand purpose, but we fail to live it out. God created us to flourish, but instead we flounder.

This is where the gospel is the answer to all human development—to all human flourishing. It is the answer because through Jesus Christ, God offers us the power to live as he created us to live—to be who he made us to be. Romans 1:16 says that the gospel "is the power of God for salvation to everyone who believes."[7]

---

2   Matthew 5:17–18.
3   John 14:12.
4   Matthew 5:48.
5   Romans 7:18–19 (NIV).
6   Romans 7:24 (NLV).
7   Romans 1:16.

We commonly understand that this *power of God for salvation* includes forgiveness of sin, a relationship with God, and the promise of eternal life. But do we also recognize that the *power of God for salvation* is for all of creation and every aspect of life?

Colossians 1:20 tells us that Christ died to reconcile to himself *all* things. All that is broken and distorted in this world by sin is to be reconciled—to be aligned with God's intentions. Mark 16:15 indicates that the gospel will affect all creation. Romans 8:21 tells us that "the creation itself will be liberated from its bondage to decay and brought into the freedom and glory of the children of God." Habakkuk 2:14 says, "For the earth will be filled with the knowledge of the glory of the Lord as the waters cover the sea."

Nonetheless, for now, the effects of sin remain. Life is difficult. The struggles and sufferings in this world continue. If God made us to flourish and to bring flourishing to our world, does the gospel—*the power of God for salvation*—have an answer for this? It does!

In Ezekiel 36:26 God says, "I will give you a new heart and put a new spirit in you." God's plan for flourishing and thriving in this world is literally putting his eternal life and Spirit into the humans he created. If heaven is where God is present, then Christ in you is heaven taking residence on this earth. Our lives become the overlap of heaven on earth.

The answer to human development and flourishing for every nation and every person is God's Spirit filling us and bringing his life to every part of our being. It is the life of God, his Spirit, that affects our day-to-day lives and gives us the ability to create the families, workplaces, communities, and nations that God intended from the beginning.

After I became a follower of Christ as a child, it took me a long time to figure this out. I understood the work of the Holy

Spirit to be that of the "sign" gifts—healing, tongues, special prophecy, or a special inner healing experience. I also knew the Holy Spirit was our helper, but I understood this to be like salt and pepper that are added to food to help preserve or improve its taste. That is, the Spirit is an ingredient shaken onto our lives when we believe, in order to give us assurance of eternal life and help us. While there is truth in this picture as far as it goes, I did not recognize that the Spirit's entrance into a life is actually more like a complete blood transfusion. The Spirit of God is not just a mere addition but the very substance and essence of our life.

Here are some ways I came to see this anew.

1. Understanding "Eternal Life"

One of the first Bible verses I memorized as a child was John 3:16: "For God so loved the world, that he gave his only begotten Son, that whosoever believeth in him should not perish, but have everlasting life" (KJV).

The promise here is *everlasting life* or, as more commonly translated, *eternal life*. Jesus speaks often about this life. Sometimes he refers to it as *eternal life* and other times simply as *life* as in the following verses (emphasis added):

- For as the Father raises the dead and gives them *life*, so also the Son gives *life* to whom he will (John 5:21).

- Yet you refuse to come to me that you may have *life* (John 5:40).

- For the bread of God is he who comes down from heaven and gives *life* to the world (John 6:33).

- The thief comes only to steal and kill and destroy. I came that they may have *life* and have it abundantly (John 10:10).

- I am the way, and the truth, and the *life*. No one comes to the Father except through me (John 14:6).

Scofield says this life is "eternal" because it is connected to the life of God, who eternally was and eternally is. It is the life of the eternal God revealed in Jesus Christ. This life of God is imparted in a new birth by the Holy Spirit. The life thus imparted is "from the beginning," but for the recipient it is a "new life" and thus makes him or her a "new creation." It is the one life of God in Christ Jesus and in the believer.[8]

Too often when we speak of having eternal life, our mind goes to life with God in heaven. But the point of having "eternal life" is that we have within us the very life of the eternal God *right now*.

2. Not Your Ordinary Life

The word *life* used by Jesus in the New Testament is the Greek word transliterated zoe.[9] It means more than just your heart beating and lungs breathing. It includes:

- the absolute fullness of life, both essential and ethical, which belongs to God, and
- life real and genuine, a life active and vigorous.

In John 10:10 Jesus makes this clear by defining this life as abundant life or life to the fullest—that is, a flourishing life.

---

8   *Scofield Study Bible NIV*, (Oxford University Press, Inc., 2004), 1674.
9   Strong's Concordance with Hebrew and Greek Lexicon, http://biblehub.com/greek/2222.htm.

3. Soaring vs. Flapping

In his book *Where Eagles Soar: Venturing with God in Tough Places,* Jamie Buckingham tells of hiking with a guide on Mount Sinai in the Sinai Peninsula.[10] At one point they stop to watch an approaching storm and spot an eagle lock its wings and catch a powerful thermal of air. The thermal carries the soaring eagle thousands of feet up and over the storm. Buckingham then refers to Isaiah 40:31 and connects the wind to the role of God's Spirit in the life of the believer: "But they that wait upon the Lord shall renew their strength; they shall mount up with wings as eagles; they shall run, and not be weary; and they shall walk, and not faint" (KJV).

This picture of an eagle with locked wings soaring through the air captured my imagination. Too often life, including the Christian life, feels more like the hummingbird outside our dining room window that has to flap its wings fifty times a second just to get around our backyard. By contrast the eagle locks its wings and soars on the wind. Isn't this God's intention for us—to fill and carry us with the wind of his Spirit amid the storms of life?

To get physical strength and to grow we drink water and eat bread. This then nurtures our physical lives. Jesus speaks of his life as living water and living bread that we can ask for and receive. His life then transforms and empowers the whole of our life.

In Ephesians 5:18 Paul wrote, "And do not get drunk with wine, for that is debauchery, but be filled with the Spirit." We are not to get drunk with wine because it alters us in a negative way. Instead we are to be filled with the Spirit, which alters us to live in the wonderful way God designed us to live.

---

10 Jamie Buckingham, *Where Eagles Soar: Venturing with God in Tough Places* (Grand Rapids: Chosen Books, 1980), 13–19.

4. Jesus's Extended Teaching on Prayer

We see another insight into the important role of the Spirit of God in human flourishing in the account of Jesus teaching his disciples to pray. The account in Matthew 6:9–13 is quite familiar to many of us, but the same teaching is recorded in Luke 11:5-13 and conveys additional instruction and insight:

> Then Jesus said to them, "Suppose you have a friend, and you go to him at midnight and say, 'Friend, lend me three loaves of bread; a friend of mine on a journey has come to me, and I have no food to offer him.' And suppose the one inside answers, 'Don't bother me. The door is already locked, and my children and I are in bed. I can't get up and give you anything.' I tell you, even though he will not get up and give you the bread because of friendship, yet because of your shameless audacity he will surely get up and give you as much as you need.
>
> "So I say to you: Ask and it will be given to you; seek and you will find; knock and the door will be opened to you. For everyone who asks receives; the one who seeks finds; and to the one who knocks, the door will be opened.
>
> "Which of you fathers, if your son asks for a fish, will give him a snake instead? Or if he asks for an egg, will give him a scorpion?
>
> "If you then, though you are evil, know how to give good gifts to your children, how much more will your Father in heaven give the Holy Spirit to those who ask him."

Jesus is teaching his followers to pray for his kingdom to come and to shamelessly and persistently ask, seek, and knock for help in the process—with the confidence that God is good and will respond accordingly.

Jesus wraps this all up by assuming that his followers *will be asking for the Holy Spirit*. For God's kingdom to come into their lives and world and for them to flourish and bring flourishing to others as God intends, they will need his life, his power, his wisdom, his mind, his living water, his bread of life, his breath, and his wind. They will need his Spirit.

The Good News of the Gospel

Paul says it this way in Ephesians 3:15–20:

> For this reason I kneel before the Father, from whom every family in heaven and on earth derives its name. I pray that out of his glorious riches he may strengthen you with power through his Spirit in your inner being, so that Christ may dwell in your hearts through faith. And I pray that you, being rooted and established in love, may have power, together with all the Lord's holy people, to grasp how wide and long and high and deep is the love of Christ, and to know this love that surpasses knowledge— *that you may be filled to the measure of all the fullness of God.* Now to him who is able to do immeasurably more than all we ask or imagine, *according to his power that is at work within us...* (emphasis added).

God's design and purpose throughout Scripture is clear. He wants to establish a residence in us, and we are to establish a residence in him. His intention is to put his life (his Spirit) into us and for our lives to be in his. In this way we become united with him.

Theologian and founder of Westminster Theological Seminary John Murray wrote that "Union with Christ is...the central truth of the whole doctrine of salvation...It is not simply a phase of the application of redemption; it underlies *every aspect* of redemption" (emphasis added).[11]

Theologian Lewis Smedes said that union with Christ is "at once the center and circumference of authentic human existence."[12]

C.S. Lewis said that "It is only the Christians who have any idea of how human souls can be taken into the life of God and yet remain themselves—in fact, be very much more themselves than they were before.... The whole purpose for which we exist is to be thus taken into the life of God."[13]

Union with Christ—God's Spirit in us—is key to living out the design God gave us at creation for the flourishing of the world and of our lives.

It is the key to flourishing!

The gospel begins in Genesis 1. It begins with God's goodness in creation and his will for all mankind to develop and enjoy this goodness and to live in relationship with him. This is the vocation he established for us at creation.

Christ's death on the cross and resurrection bring forgiveness for sin, hope for heaven, and a personal relationship with God. It *also* enables us to live out our vocation in this broken and difficult world. Through Christ's atonement God puts his life—the Spirit of Christ—into us, giving us his desire, wisdom, and power to live as he designed us to live. This is good news!

This is how the gospel connects to development and flourishing. This is God's plan for every individual, community, and nation.

---

11 John Murray, *Redemption—Accomplished and Applied* (Eerdmans, 1955), 201, 205.
12 Lewis Smedes, *Union with Christ*, (Eerdmans, 1983), xii.
13 C.S. Lewis, *Mere Christianity*, (MacMillan, 1952) 127, 128.

God has put *you* on this earth at this particular time in history both to flourish and to bring flourishing to his world. This is not easy, but it is always possible through the Spirit of Christ in us.

Have you trusted in Christ and his full payment for your sin? Are you asking and relying on him to fill you with his Spirit each day, to reveal his word to you, and give you the ability to live as he created you to live? If not, why not start now?

The world awaits.

> But blessed is the one who trusts in the Lord,
> whose confidence is in him.
> They will be like a tree planted by the water
> that sends out its roots by the stream.
> It does not fear when heat comes;
> its leaves are always green.
> It has no worries in a year of drought
> and never fails to bear fruit.
>
> *—Jeremiah 17:7–8*

About the Author

Dwight Vogt serves as the vice president of international programs for the Disciple Nations Alliance (DNA). Before coming to the DNA, he worked for 27 years at Food for the Hungry, including field-based leadership roles in Thailand, Bangladesh and Peru. Dwight is the author of *Footings for Children: Imparting a Biblical Worldview So They Can Thrive*. He earned his master's degree in intercultural studies and missiology from Biola University. He has three adult children and lives with his wife, Deborah, in Phoenix. You can contact Dwight at info@disciplenations.org

Disciple Nations Alliance (www.disciplenations.org) is a movement that exists to help the church rise to her full potential as God's principal agent in the restoration, healing, and blessing of broken nations. We accomplish our purpose by equipping God's people to be the hands and feet of Jesus in their families, communities, and through their vocations.

Our vision is to envision churches with a biblical worldview and equip them to practice a wholistic, incarnational ministry affecting all spheres of society. We provide simple tools that enable churches to begin the transformation process immediately, with existing resources – no matter how materially poor they may be.

If you would like more information about the Disciple Nations Alliance or our teaching and training resources, please visit our website.

Disciple Nations Alliance
1110 E. Missouri Ave., Suite 393
Phoenix, AZ 85014
www.disciplenations.org

Made in the USA
Lexington, KY
03 December 2019

58067308R00051